Making a Difference

RESPECTING
Our World

Sue Barraclough

W
FRANKLIN WATTS
LONDON · SYDNEY

First published in 2006 by
Franklin Watts
338 Euston Road
London NW1 3BH

Franklin Watts Australia
Level 17/207 Kent Street
Sydney NSW 2000

© 2006 Franklin Watts

Original concept devised by
Sue Barraclough and Jemima Lumley.

Editor: Adrian Cole
Designer: Jemima Lumley
Art director: Jonathan Hair
Special photography: Mark Simmons (except where listed below)
Consultant: Helen Peake, Education Officer at
  The Recycling Consortium, Bristol

Acknowledgements:
The author and publisher wish to thank Helen Peake and the staff at
The Recycling Consortium. FSC logo © Forest Stewardship Council A. C.
reproduced by kind permission: 11. Coast Originals: 9bl, br, photographer
Paul Abbitt, ring designed by Bea Reseigh and mugs by Alice Harwood
© Coast Originals. Remarkable Pencils Ltd (www.remarkable.co.uk): 11c, 27tr.
Ben Dickens (www.bensbirdboxes.com): 17. Barrie Watts: 15b. Images on
pages 7cl, 19br, 21bl, 27br supplied by the national Recycle Now campaign
(for more information on recycling visit www.recyclenow.com). The children
and parents from Sefton Park School, Bristol: 23tl, bl. Andy Crawford: 20.
Chris Fairclough: 23br. © Digital Vision 6–7b, 7tl, 8c, 9tr, 10, 22. Townsed P.
Dickinson/Image Works/Topfoto: 12cr. Eastcott-Momatiuk/Topfoto: 16.

Special thanks to Connie, James, Romi, Ruby and Tom for taking part.

A CIP catalogue record for this book is available
from the British Library.

ISBN: 978 0 7496 6485 5
Dewey Classification: 333.7

Printed in China

Franklin Watts is a division of Hachette Children's Books,
an Hachette Livre UK company.

Contents

Our world

Our world gives us water to drink and air to breathe. It gives us materials and fuels. Plants grow in the soil to make the food we eat. We must respect and look after our world.

Air to breathe

Water to drink

Materials to make things

Fuels for cooking and heating

Soil to grow things

Food to eat

Natural materials

Some materials we use to make things are dug out of the ground. Some materials grow in the ground. Wood from trees can be used to make toys, paper and furniture.

A wooden toy

Paper

A wooden chair

Oil is taken from deep under the ground to make plastic. Some bottles are made from plastic. Oil is also used to make fuel for cars.

Did you know?

All the materials used to make these things come from the ground.

A glass jar

A steel can

A silver ring

Pottery cups

All about trees

Trees give us wood to make things,
such as furniture and paper. They
make clean air for us to breathe, too.

Trees also provide homes and food
for many animals. We all need trees
so people must take care of them.

If a tree is cut down to make something, a new tree should be planted in its place. The FSC make sure forests around the world are well looked after.

What you can do

When you buy things made from wood look out for the FSC sign.

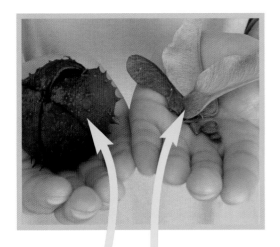

Tree seeds

Look out for tree seeds in gardens or parks. Then try planting them in a pot of soil. Seeds need sunlight and water to make them grow.

Leave only footprints

Rubbish can be dangerous to animals. If we leave rubbish behind it pollutes our world.

If you go to the park for a picnic, do not leave any rubbish behind. Leave only footprints!

Take your rubbish
home with you.
It's easy to do.
Drinks cans can
be recycled,
and you may
be able to reuse
other things.

What you can do

Some picnic things,
such as plastic knives
and forks, cups and
bottles, can be reused.

Nature's recyclers

If you know where to look, you can find lots of recycling creatures, such as slugs, snails and worms. One of the best places to look is in a compost bin.

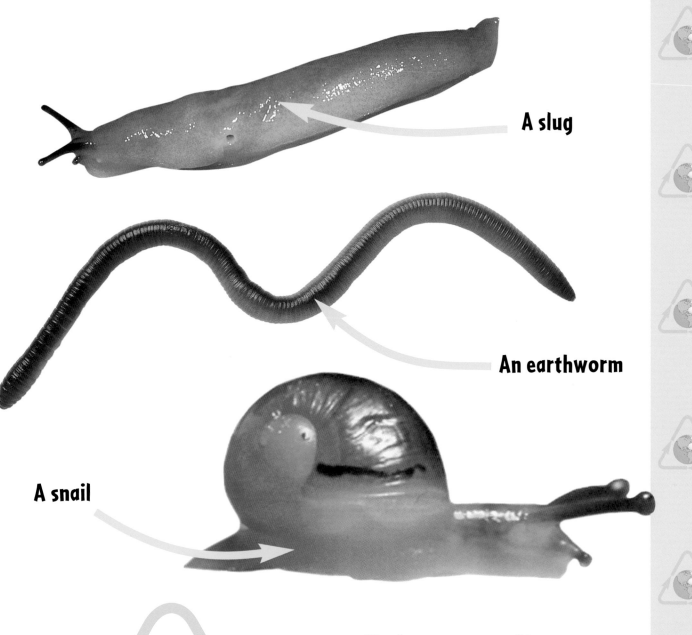

A slug

An earthworm

A snail

All these recycling creatures are busy eating the food waste in the compost bin. They help to break the waste down into compost. It is used to help plants grow.

Homes and food

We all need somewhere to live and food to eat. When people build houses and farms, many animals lose their homes and may not find enough food to eat.

You can help some animals, such as birds. You can make them a home, and put out food for them to eat.

Ask a grown-up to help you make a simple nesting box. This one is made from a reused 'For Sale' board.

You can put out food for birds. Many birds eat stale bread and nuts.

What you can do

Make sure that you put nesting boxes and bird feeders in a safe place. Hang bird feeders high up. Put nesting boxes in places where cats cannot reach them.

We should put out more food for birds in the winter, when there is less around for them to eat.

Saving water

Rain falls from the clouds in the sky and fills streams and rivers. This water is stored in reservoirs.

It is cleaned and then pumped along pipes to our homes.

Drinking water

Watering a plant

All living things need water, and we use huge amounts every day. Clean, fresh water is very precious. We need to respect how important it is, and not waste it.

What you can do to save water

Turn off the tap while you brush your teeth.

Ask an adult to mend any dripping taps.

Have a shower instead of a bath.

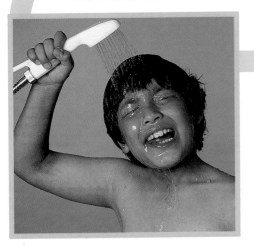

If you have a garden, collect rainwater in a water butt to water the plants.

Saving energy

Many of the things we use, such as lights, televisions, heaters and computers, need energy to make them work. Most of the energy comes from burning natural materials.

We burn oil, gas and coal.
We need to save energy
because one day
these fuels will run
out. Burning fuels
also pollutes
our air.

What you can do to save energy

Turn off your
computer when you
have finished.
Do not leave TVs and
stereos on standby.

Switch
off lights
in empty
rooms.

Use energy-
saving
lightbulbs in
your home.

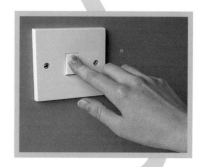

Clean air

We use cars to travel around. But most car engines use up lots of fuel and pump out poisonous fumes. These pollute the air we breathe.

There are other ways to travel around. We can help to keep the air clean by using these instead of cars.

What you can do

Find out if your school has a pick-up service, called a 'walking bus'.

Ride a bicycle

Catch a bus

Walk

Saving our world

We can all help to save our world. If we reduce our rubbish, reuse things and recycle materials we won't use so many natural materials. But we must also help to save energy and water, and cut down on pollution.

What you can do

Put less rubbish into your bin by reducing, reusing and recycling rubbish.

Think of ways to reuse things, like these yoghurt pots that have been made into plant pots

Reduce your rubbish by choosing loose vegetables without packaging

Sort materials and recycle them

What is it made from?

We waste lots of materials when we throw them away. These things are made from materials that can be reused or recycled.

Can you name all the materials? Look back through the book if you need help.

1

2

3

4

Answers on page 29.

Make a difference quiz

How much do you know about respecting our world?

Try to answer all of these questions on a sheet of scrap paper.

1. In what four ways can you help to save water?

2. What should you take home after a picnic in the park?

3. What four things can you do to help save energy?

4. Name three recycling creatures.

5. How can we travel around, without using a car?

Find out more

If we respect our world we are more likely to take good care of it. We also need to reduce our waste and make sure that we save resources such as water, energy and natural materials. The websites below will help you to find out more about respecting our world.

www.est.org.uk/myhome
Tips, ideas and quizzes on saving energy.

www.panda.org
The World Wildlife Fund website. Follow the links to the education section for information on saving wildlife and habitats.

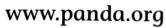

www.greenpeace.org/international
and
www.foe.co.uk/living/quiz
Two websites full of ideas on saving the planet.

www.planetark.com
Your daily guide to helping the planet.

www.ollierecycles.com/planet
Fun, facts and information on saving the planet.

www.yptenc.org.uk
The Young People's Trust for the Environment – includes factsheets on a range of topics from building a birdhouse to making paper. With useful links to a range of other websites to find out even more.

www.rspb.org.uk/youth
A fantastic site for wildlife explorers, with lots to do, make and discover.

Every effort has been made by the Publishers to ensure that these websites contain no inappropriate or offensive material. However, because of the nature of the Internet, it is impossible to guarantee that the contents of these sites will not be altered. We strongly advise that Internet access is supervised by a responsible adult.

Glossary

Compost – plant materials that have broken down. People use compost to help plants grow.

Compost bin – a container used to store kitchen and garden waste where it breaks down to make compost.

FSC – the Forest Stewardship Council saves areas of natural forest and makes sure that forests are well looked after.

Fuel – something that can be used to produce light and heat, and to work machines.

Material – the substance something is made from.

Pollute – to make dirty or poison something.

Recycle – if you recycle something, you use it again or make it into something new.

Reservoir – a large lake used to store water.

Resources – things that we take from our world such as water, materials to make things and fuels to create energy.

Reuse – to use something again.

Answers to quiz on page 26: 1 – the jar is made of glass, which is made mainly from a special type of sand; 2 – the duck is made of wood taken from trees; 3 – the can is made from a metal called steel, which is dug out of the ground; 4 – the paper is made from wood from trees.

Index

About this book

Making A Difference: Respecting Our World aims to encourage children to think about their world. The main aim is to encourage children to think about their impact on the planet, and to help them see that they can make a difference to their environment.

Page 8 looks at the materials that we get from the Earth. Encourage children to look at objects and discover what they are made from.
Page 10 focuses on the importance of trees to a healthy planet. Look at trees in parks and gardens, draw attention to sizes and shapes. Try growing a tree from seed.
Use page 14 to encourage children to notice how Nature recycles natural materials.
Page 16 could be used to introduce the idea of habitats, and to talk about the importance of wildlife in our world.
Use page 18 to think about where water comes from and how vital it is to all living things.
Page 20 looks at energy and how important it is to almost every aspect of our lives. Encourage children to think about alternative sources of energy.
Use page 22 to look at how many of us rely on cars, but discuss the idea that there are many other ways of getting around that are healthier.